ZOË'S CATS

The Sniffer

Zoë Stokes

ZOË'S CATS

with 32 color plates

THAMES AND HUDSON

The Sniffer

When I was painting this picture, I think every cat in the neighbourhood must have come to sample the aromatic delights of the catmint in our front garden. One by one they stumbled up the brick path with their nostrils flared, gradually flattening a once-bushy plant into the soil with the weight of their appreciative bodies.

Some cats rolled in it, purring loudly. Others lay in it, motionless. The most amusing characters were those that sat in unusual positions inhaling until their bodies swayed, ecstatic and intoxicated.

© 1982 Thames and Hudson Limited, London

First published in the USA in 1982 by Thames and Hudson Inc., 500 Fifth Avenue New York, New York 10110

Library of Congress Catalog Card Number 81-53055

Printed and bound in Japan

The Distraction

Years ago, Sam and Mungo were playmates. Immediately after breakfast Mungo would run up the lane to Sam's home and sit on the kitchen window sill, his face pressed against the glass, waiting for his friend's release.

Occasionally Sam would be the first to surface, and the sudden appearance of his two wicked blue eyes at our kitchen window often startled me. His presence also encouraged Mungo to gorge his food even faster than usual, resulting in a bad attack of hiccoughs.

Once united, they made straight for the fields. They enjoyed playing games like hide-and-seek, usually following the human rules but sometimes inventing a new version in which the hidden party, bored with waiting to be found, jumped out on his unprepared partner.

This friendship brought great joy to both cats but it changed Sam's habits; his previously predictable nature became unreliable and when he forgot to return home punctually at meal times, his owners worried. They clattered his saucers, and called his name across the fields.

In this painting, I imagined Sam and Mungo playing in the fields, the last bright yellow burst of evening sunshine on their coats. Stopping mid-tumble, turning their heads towards the cluster of cottages where we live, they are distracted for a moment by the clink of saucers or an anxious voice carried on clear Cornish air.

 Sunday Afternoons

This is a portrait of someone I know, at home on a Sunday afternoon. At least, it's how I imagine him – numerous chores and intended healthful walks forgotten in the comfort of a favourite armchair. New Year's resolutions superseded by a large tasty lunch, a quiet read and an occasional snooze.

I couldn't remember the view from his window, so I painted ours instead, showing the cottages across the lane, part of our front garden and the thatched bird-tray which has since been blown naked by gale-force winds.

Last Orders
(overleaf)

When I look at certain people I see animals and sometimes animals make me think of people. This habit started during my childhood and has never left me. I noticed cats' expressions were particularly like our own, and saw in their personalities reflections of people I had met; friends, neighbours, passing strangers, even myself at times!

During my early twenties, I applied for the position of barmaid at a sports club. I was there only for a few short months, but this painting stemmed from that invaluable experience.

These characters are not meant to be members of that club; this is an imaginary country inn with its melting pot of customers.

The ginger-and-white habitué on the far left is Mungo, one of our family: once a half-wild kitten, now a temperamental adult. He spends most of his time out of doors, returning home thirsty and impatient after a day in the fields. His manners are appalling. He guzzles his drink at remarkable speed, licks the dribbles off his white bib, then lies down to recover from flatulence.

Waiting

As well as Mungo, we have a tabby-pointed Siamese called Twiggy. She's a nosy little lady who spends many pleasurable hours perched on top of the biscuit tin in the kitchen.

From this rather unstately pedestal she watches people passing in the lane, stretching her neck until they disappear. Or she calls to the birds in the garden. This sound makes me think of a partly strangled witch, trying to laugh. Her lips quiver, her tail thrashes from side to side, and eventually her whole body wobbles with so much excitement that she slips off her perch.

Although Twiggy's funny ways gave me the idea for this picture, I decided to paint a different type of Siamese cat enjoying a view of Gwithian, a nearby village that nestles between fields and sand dunes.

We live on the boundary of Gwithian Parish, so I sometimes walk down to the village with our youngest dog for company, going via back-tracks and lanes and returning home up this hill, which is the coast road. It makes a lovely walk, especially in June when the showy poppies gently sway above the still fresh green of the grassy banks.

Quiet Moments

Here's Twiggy cat-napping while the rest of the family are in the garden. Not properly asleep, conscious enough to purr occasionally, yet so relaxed that even her ears have gone limp and droop sideways. When she lies like this, with her legs curled in front, she adopts the position a neighbour so aptly describes as 'cuddling her hot water bottles'.

Like most cats, Twiggy is a menace where knitting is concerned. A piece of abandoned knitting in a chair immediately tempts her to create a nest out of it. Turning round and round to make a hollow of the correct cat-like proportions, she manages to bend the needles, drop the stitches and kick the ball of wool onto the floor where it becomes a new toy for a surprised little dog.

❧ Excess Baggage ❧

Twiggy was six months old when we brought her home to join our family. She was undersized for her age, with legs like sticks; hence her name.

She didn't want to play at all. My mother and I tied bits of paper onto string and pranced around the room trying to encourage her to follow, but she just sat there purring. She preferred to investigate the cottage and all its contents. Cats are of course curious by nature, but Twiggy's investigations were absurd. She singed her whiskers sniffing at candles, burnt her head by peering into a hot oven, and nearly drowned herself by diving into a bathful of water.

A less dangerous pastime was sifting through the contents of my handbag.

16

🍀 The Treasure Hunt 🍀

During my childhood we had a small blue-grey cat called Bobo whose litters were amazingly pretty considering the undesirable characters she chose to father them. I was delighted, whatever they looked like, insisting that even the ugliest had its own kind of beauty.

My normal reluctance to go to school changed to a positive loathing with the arrival of kittens; every minute away from them meant the possibility of missing another stage in their development – perhaps the moment they opened their eyes or began the initial stages of play, and later on the first clumsy pounce or amusing game of chase. When they were old enough, I encouraged them to explore the various objects on top of my dressing-table, while I watched their amusing reactions.

❧ December Washday ❧

Like most cats, Mungo has a built-in barometer which enables him to return home from his expeditions before the arrival of bad weather. Nevertheless, during the winter months he often comes indoors dripping with mud from trampling over sodden fields, and his wet coat – which I suspect has literally been dragged through a hedge backwards – conceals all kinds of peculiar souvenirs from his travels.

Among his collection there have been caterpillars, stick-insects, slugs, snails, and spiders' webs that hang from broken twigs (occasionally still intact with occupant). Strange heads suddenly appear from beneath his fur in the warmth of the cottage, rising and swaying as they attempt to crawl to freedom.

If we notice his arrival we try to rub him down with an old towel, but his aggressive nature can make this dangerous. He allows the excess moisture to be removed from his head and back, providing this is done in a gentle stroking action while he drinks his milk, but intentionally helpful hands that try to disentangle matted fur or dry other areas of his body are swiftly rejected by a sharp hefty paw. Then he glares threateningly, ears held horizontal, in case we try to interfere with him again.

He prefers to wash himself unaided and does an excellent job of it, too. It never ceases to amaze me how he can transform his filthy, stringy coat into clean dry fluffiness using only his tiny pink tongue, his teeth and saliva.

This painting shows Mungo's return home last December when the darkening sky forecast oncoming rain. The view through the window is based on our own, looking towards Pulsack Manor, but not showing the lane that separates our front garden from the fields.

Sunshine in February

This is my impression of our next-door neighbour, who lives on the other side of the bank that features so much in our cats' lives. He's the one on the right, pictured talking to a friend in the sheltered doorway of his garden shed. Both had their faces turned towards the warmth of the sun on a particularly bright February day.

This neighbour and his wife are not cat owners but they show great tolerance towards their feline visitors – namely Mungo, Twiggy and Sam – who sometimes take advantage of their hospitality. For example, Twiggy blotted her copy-book by curling up on their cold frame, stretching the plastic windows with the weight of her warm body until they sunk inwards.

These short trips next door are as exciting as a world tour to Twiggy; she returns home ten minutes later with her fur standing upright and her eyes wide with surprise while she exaggerates all her experiences. She invents things as well – she swears they keep a hippopotamus in the water garden and keeps running back to the window to make sure nothing has followed her home.

Sam is thoroughly spoilt. His Lordship has been provided with a specially reserved, cloth-lined seed box which is placed in the shed doorway so that he can sunbathe like his human friends. Not too far forward, not too far back; yes, just there; that will do nicely, thank you.

Mungo is far too suspicious to relax like the others, but he does use our neighbours' garden as a short cut to the adjacent field, and he has been accused of stopping long enough to use the well-dug flower beds for personal reasons.

Signs of Spring

Down one side of our garden there is a high bank which divides our land from our next-door neighbour's and helps to shelter us from the east winds. It used to be topped with an attractive line of leafy elm trees, but now all that remains are ivy-covered skeletons which serve as nesting places for the crows and probably shelter for some of the bats that I see flying around at night.

Early in the year, periwinkle grows wild along the top of this bank, between the trees. When I see these splashes of blue after the winter I feel that spring is really on the way.

Another sign of the forthcoming season is the reappearance of Twiggy's fan club, a multi-coloured selection of hopeful tomcats that lie amid the periwinkle, waiting for a glimpse of our little lady as she tiptoes around the garden. I don't know why they bother – she's more interested in the damp grass, delicately lifting each paw high and shaking off any offending drops of moisture as though she had trodden in something nasty. Perhaps she thinks her paws will dissolve.

I decided to paint one of these admirers. This one was particularly keen to make her acquaintance and thumped the ground with a furry boot to attract her attention. Obviously not the right approach for Twiggy, who was so horrified she scrambled through the open kitchen window with her tail fanned out like a brush.

Caught in the Act

Apart from her nosiness and clumsiness, Twiggy has a sweet and gentle nature, usually behaving submissively towards the other animals, and never scratches a human being intentionally. She might use a slightly extended claw to attract our attention but she has never been known to strike an

aggressive blow. Even if we accidentally tread on her tail she only miaows and looks upward woefully.

Nevertheless, there is a destructive side to her character. Apart from tearing wallpaper, she has a love-hate relationship with flowers. She loves their smell; especially the highly perfumed varieties such as my mother's prized lillium, from which she emerges with tell-tale blobs of pollen on her head. It's the flowers with small petals and short stems that she mutilates, tapping them softly with her paw until they drop like confetti. She watches this with her ears forward, head on one side – ooooh, isn't it pretty! Alternatively, she removes the petals one by one with her teeth, spitting them over her shoulder in a rather noisy fashion.

This picture illustrates Twiggy's reaction when we ask her what she's doing. Once again, not a painting of Twiggy – but she was responsible for the idea.

Momentary Madness

I tend to use Twiggy a lot in my paintings – not only as she is, but also in disguise. Yet it occurred to me that I usually paint Mungo as himself, wearing his ginger-and-white coat in varying degrees of cleanliness. I suppose the reason for this is quite simple if I stop to analyse.

Twiggy rarely strays further than our next-door neighbour's garden, occuping most of her time fiddling around indoors. This gives me the opportunity to sketch and study her funny ways, of which there are so many that I would get bored painting them all into one body, so I paint them into the bodies of other cats.

Twiggy is also an excellent model. Because she is short-coated her body movements are easy to see and she's most co-operative if I want to study, in detail, various parts of her anatomy! Therefore, both consciously and unconsciously on my part, she finds her way into many of my paintings.

This picture is the result of a collection of quick sketches of Twiggy's movements during one of her mad moments. I love to watch the performance of a natural Siamese gymnast: leaping, boxing the air, chasing her tail – her ears at odd angles, her eyes glazed with insanity and her head full of imaginings.

❧ The Family Album ❧

All Siamese cat owners are only too aware of the variation of sounds their pet can produce from its larynx.

Before Twiggy's arrival, I had never met a cat with such a comprehensive vocabulary or such hyperactive vocal cords. I have already attempted to describe one of these sounds – her amusing call to the birds – but there are also some extremely aggravating noises.

Most of these are included in what is best described as a Siamese monologue: a boring performance all about her longing for a saucer of tinned fish dinner even though she has just filled herself with mushy biscuits. It consists of one act, in three parts, opening with the notorious Siamese wail.

To produce the wail Twiggy thrusts her head forward, opens her mouth wide, and the dreadful noise continues until all breath has left her body.

She refills her lungs while waiting for audience reaction. We decide to ignore her and walk away, so she follows quickly with the siren. This weird sound is produced by wailing while she runs back and forth like someone most impatiently trying to hail a taxi on a busy evening. This is unbearable. I rush to open a tin quickly and frequently cut myself on the lid. That's when I hear her raucous laugh – the final part of her performance. It's a cross between a chuckle and a gravelly miaow, and was initially responsible for this picture.

Alarm Clocks with Legs

Back to the peace and quiet of Cornwall, early morning. I'm in bed. The dark veil of sleep has just lifted from underneath my closed eyelids and my ears have begun to function enough to realize that I have been wakened by an automobile engine roaring away in the bedroom.

Slowly, as I return to consciousness, I discover it's only Twiggy vibrating the bed while she purrs her morning greeting. Warm and comfortable, I continue to feign sleep. Disappointed by my lack of response, she tries tickling my face with her whiskers, taps my nose with her paw and purrs a loud reveille in my ear. I still remain a motionless lump beneath blankets.

This gives me about one minute of peaceful bliss before she returns with her willing accomplice, Chico. All too soon I hear the sound of eight paws galloping along the landing and brace myself for the onslaught – a cat in the chest and a dog in the stomach. A most painful experience.

Nevertheless, I must not wince; if I can restrain myself they will leave me alone for a bit longer and chase each other round the bed instead. It works, they finally settle, and I wonder what kind of expression Chico has this morning. Forewarned is forearmed.

Carefully, I peer through half-opened eyes. Certainly not a sweet-tempered wide-eyed teddy bear. Nor a tousled mischievous Willum. Nor even a pinched mean-eyed short-tempered foxy face. He has his positively rabid look. Today will obviously be one of those crazy days.

That's done it. My eyelids moved, and he noticed. He has begun to strip the bed, layer by layer, bouncing around so much it feels as though I lie on a cold choppy sea.

When I open my eyes I see a huge paw ready to pat my face. Behind that, two colossal blue eyes staring out of Twiggy's head. Behind her, a little mad dog rises from the bottom of the bed ready to leap. A long tongue drips between his sharp teeth and his one visible *eye* is fixed on my face.

This means I have precisely one second to throw myself sideways onto the floor before he reaches the top of the bed and licks me to death. . . .

The Smithy, Kehelland

This place fascinates me with its peeling paintwork, corrugated roof and rusty bolts.

Inside, the walls are decorated with innumerable tools; interesting shapes for intricate wrought-iron work, heavy chisels and hammers for shoeing. There seem to be horseshoes everywhere – some balanced neatly on nails in rows, others lying on the floor in little piles or hanging over the sides of already filled boxes. Bits of soiled straw blow across the floor in the breeze.

All these things combined with the amazing skill of the blacksmith – the echo as the hammer shapes the shoe upon the anvil and the unique steamy smell of hot iron united with hoof – create a special atmosphere. I thought a cat, startled by the activity, would complete the picture.

Sadly, perhaps ironically, this building could be demolished in a year or two to make way for a new major highway. It may not have a quaint picture-postcard appearance but it is another small piece of local history that will vanish forever, along with the huge pile of worn and discarded shoes that at present stand like a monument in the rough grass outside.

Cats in the Calf House

The next three paintings portray the cats from a nearby farm, now called Pulsack Manor but originally part of a large area shown as 'Pulza' on an early nineteenth-century map.

The front of our cottage overlooks some of its 143 acres of good arable land, and the farmstead itself is approached by a tree-lined track that leads off the lane where we live.

I love the old beamed barns, the attractive house with its interesting past, the wildlife in the hedges that surround the peaceful fields, and of course the animals, which include the farm cats of many shapes, sizes and colours. However, I soon discovered that farm cats are not the most accommodating subjects to sketch and study. Apart from Ginger and Snowy, who were hand-fed when their mother met with a fatal accident, the other cats think vehicles are harmless but two-legged strangers are to be distrusted and preferably avoided altogether.

Lad, the farm's Welsh collie, didn't help. Jealous of the attention the cats were receiving, he waited until I managed to creep within sketching distance of a sleeping mass of wild feline bodies, then came bounding forward, playfully scattering them in all directions before chasing them off into the distance.

Eventually I decided there were only two means of watching them unnoticed and undisturbed; one was by sitting in the comfort of the car and the other by concealing myself in the straw in one of the sheds or barns where the various noises and smells from the other creatures would hopefully disguise my presence.

Entering the calf house I was fascinated by the cobwebs that hung round the window frame like miniature fishing nets, and intrigued by the yards of crimson twine that secured the water pipes to the old wooden stalls.

Finding an empty stall I shut myself in and waited for the cats to enter through the small hole in the wall and the broken window pane.

The first cat to appear was Ginger, his impudent face adorned with bits of straw. He was quickly followed by others who either played or slept in the troughs, surprising me by showing no fear of the calves at all. In fact, the calves were more wary of the cats.

🍀 The Mousers, at Work 🍀

When I entered this old barn I interrupted a few cats that were busy hunting for mice amid the straw. Most of them fled almost immediately, but the fluffy black-and-white remained, peeping shyly from behind a bale – until Lad came gamboling along and chased the poor thing up a beam. These cats are all nameless, apart from the short-coated black-and-white, who is called Snowy. Well, we don't see much snow in Cornwall!

I decided to try and paint my impression of them mousing, as if I had been watching from the back of the barn, showing the view through the alcove across the tranquil farmyard when all the men were in the fields. The bales at the front glittered like gold in the sunlight and the delightful smell of clean warm straw filled the air.

The Farmyard Scrum

Pulsack Manor has been in the possession of the Hosking family since 1921, and is now farmed by the fourth generation. As in 1921, the farm still carries a large herd of Friesian cattle and every morning, after milking, the cats gather round the back porch to wait for their breakfast.

It's a pretty sight as they all trot behind Mrs Hosking to the milking parlour with their assorted tails held like furry question marks above their backs; short ones, long ones, thin, fluffy and fat. Waiting on the steps outside, they miaow impatiently until their large dish is filled with fresh milk and placed before them in the yard.

This picture illustrates the mad scramble as they all try to drink at once. The successful splash each other's faces with droplets of milk as they lap while the timid queue patiently with down-turned mouths and anxious eyes.

The numbers vary daily; this particular morning there were fifteen but I added the fluffy black-and-white behind the old tire because of the way she had peeped at me in the barn.

The False Prediction

It was nearing the end of October and I was doodling while I listened on the radio to a programme about Hallowe'en. Afterwards I looked at what I had drawn and the basic idea amused me enough to continue with it.

Initially, there were only two characters: the fortune teller with a crystal ball and the character on the right whose mouth was open. The latter just had to be Twiggy – though I'm not sure if she's screaming with fright or gasping with delight. Even so, knowing how nervous she can be when she ventures out alone, especially at night, I thought it only fair to give her a friend for support.

A Korat cat would probably make an ideal companion for such an occasion, considering some people believe they bring good luck. Not only that – luminous green eyes between large leafy plants and a silver-tipped coat in front of the window appealed to me.

Then I decided the fortune teller should have an air of mystery, like the beautiful Birman whose unusual colouring is surrounded by legend. I thought striking dark points would also emphasize the intense expression in the one visible eye that studies poor Twiggy's reaction to the Tall Dark Stranger.

The Fly That Got By

Over the years I have tried to sketch some of the movements and expressions that are included in the fast and fascinating turnabout that cats sometimes do when a fly dares to come within striking distance. Not actually chasing the insect but simply trying to catch it as it passes, the cat rarely finishes more than twelve inches from its initial position.

The turnabout consists of many supple and energetic movements, yet the whole sequence lasts only a couple of seconds, often leaving me with just an impression: a confused but beautiful memory of whirls of action and coat pattern, especially from the cats who have tabby markings.

Thinking about this impression and imagining the tabby markings as watermarks in Eastern silks – the way their name originated – I continued to form this picture with pattern foremost in my mind, choosing six sketches from my collection of turnabout movements which I thought might make an attractive design when grouped together.

These six sketches begin on the left with The Sighting, where the cat's neck stretches while its head rotates with the path of the approaching fly.

The two middle exercises, The Sitting Swipe and The Grab, are Mungo's favourite movements, displaying a tremendous amount of aggressive concentration as he tries to crush his catch between powerful paws.

Twiggy is best at The Leap and The Peep. In fact Twiggy's Peep is practised far too often for a successful record and her nosy nature is always the cause of her losing the catch.

Which leads to the final position on the right, where the cat watches the escaping fly with an expression best described as The Silent Snarl, which is usually followed by a pretend sneeze, another unnecessary wash or a haughty toss of the head.

Cat with a Cue

When a cat creeps slowly towards a ping-pong ball it reminds me of a billiards player about to strike; both consider angle, distance and reaction with the same expressive mixture of determination and concentration.

Influenced by the television coverage of this fascinating sport, I gave this character a smart black waistcoat and imagined that I was behind a camera, closely following every move of a professional performance.

The background was in darkness, there was silence apart from the commentator's hushed voice, the bright overhead light shone onto the player's body which in turn cast dark shadows across the velvety green baize as he positioned his cue at just the right angle and. . . .

I fear that enthusiasts and professionals will quickly recognize that I know very little indeed about the techniques of playing billiards, but it was the cat's expression that really interested me.

The Twenty Minute Tale

When I begin the group paintings that amalgamate people and animals, I seldom have a clear idea of what the finished picture will be like. I just have fun, allowing them to take shape while I'm sketching.

For example, I might start with someone I've seen or met, then another comes into mind, followed by an incident, until eventually a whole picture forms. Then I tidy it up. I say 'tidy it up', but really I get into an awful mess; rubbing out certain characters, adding others, thinking of balance and trying not to repeat past mistakes. By the time the sketch is finished I have pencil marks up to my elbows, an overworked eraser and a piece of paper with holes in it where I've had a spot of trouble.

The principal character in this painting is one of those people who grabs hold of you while they talk, slapping you across the shoulder blades every so often to keep you awake. He had to be Siamese: they have so much to say.

I wanted to surround him with more characters, so I put him in a bar situation. I fancied painting a seedy looking joint, where the bar would be dripping with slops, the notice brown with tobacco and curled with age. Even the pink elephant would be on his last legs, affected by the fumes from the rotting meat pies and exhausted by the tedious length of the tale.

Tarzan in a June Jungle

This picture was painted to emphasize Mungo's remarkable zest for life as he leaps like another version of Tarzan from the overgrown bank to surprise us; often yelling with pleasure before crash-landing in the forget-me-nots.

About four years ago Mungo left home after breakfast to go on one of his regular expeditions with Sam – or so we thought. This time, however, he didn't return in the evening for his dinner, and when he didn't appear the following day either, we began to worry.

Sam's owners said they hadn't seen him. Neither had our next-door neighbours – who very kindly helped us search all the places we knew he favoured for hunting and sleeping, with no result.

After a week, worried but still reasonably optimistic about his safety, I telephoned the nearest stray cats refuge, thinking someone might have found him and taken him there; but no.

After a month of futile inquiries at various animal organizations, we gave up hope. Then one morning, when my mother opened the back door to let the dogs into the garden, a thin, tired, filthy, flea-ridden version of Mungo walked in. You can imagine how we felt, each taking turns to greet him and hold him several times over – fleas as well!

Three days later, clean, flea-less and refreshed, he resumed his normal activities, leaving home in the morning and returning at night to eat.

Then, on the afternoon of the fourth day, my mother found him crawling across the front garden covered in blood and obviously in great pain. We never learnt what had happened, but assumed from his injuries that he had been hit by some kind of vehicle.

We called the vet and did all we could to make Mungo comfortable, but during the first few days he was in such a bad state that we seriously considered having him humanely destroyed. I'm so glad we didn't, for although it was a long convalescence he slowly regained his former strength and eventually resumed an active life exploring the fields and hunting, as before.

1981

❧ Tables for Two ❧

Welcome to the Cat's Whisker Restaurant – imaginary purveyors of good food and wine, where you can enjoy a candlelit dinner accompanied by soft background music in luxurious surroundings. Unfortunately, the service is unusually slow tonight due to a few minor problems.

At table six, the character who has just been served with what he considers to be a poor wine is struggling to find the words to say so. A normally self-assertive man, he wonders why he crumbles with inferiority in front of a wine waiter, and nervously fiddles with his cutlery while he searches for the best solution to this nightmare-come-true. How will the waiter react if he complains, and what will his companion think of him if he doesn't?

Table four is attended by a most unhappy man; his elastic bow tie snapped earlier on in the evening and had to be refastened three inches shorter, restricting his breathing. His back aches and his legs throb. He doesn't think he will last much longer. Any minute now he expects to collapse headlong into the vase of flowers and wonders if the customers will continue to discuss their order over his dead body. He recommends the lobster in a quiet refined voice. But they don't reply. *Heigh-ho.* While he waits, he dreams of home – the comfort a bucketful of hot water will bring to his aching feet.

On to table five, where Twiggy and Mungo are about to begin their dessert course. It will be a long time before this table becomes vacant; Mungo's greed and adventurous nature have encouraged him to order a huge Knickerbocker Glory topped with a pink sugar mouse. While he journeys into its depths Twiggy will show her usual disgust at his bad manners. When at home she tries to avoid watching him eat. Everyone does. It's not a pretty sight.

Cosy table seven will be occupied for the rest of the evening by an ardent suitor who is desperately trying to declare his love between courses. Overcome by emotion, he knocks over his wine while his companion's elbow rests on a bread roll.

The most peculiar interview I ever attended began with a long journey on a cold, dismal day. Upon my arrival, I was directed to a large upstairs room where I had to wait, with many others, for my name to be called from an adjacent office. The more experienced applicants had brought something to read; the rest of us either stared at the potted plants or scrutinized each other. The room was dreadfully hot.

It was then I discovered the hook on the back of my dress had become firmly attached to my coat. I was struggling to separate the two, one arm down my back underneath my clothes, when my prospective employer called me into the office.

Still overdressed and the colour of a boiled lobster, I followed him into his little oven. Rolling up his shirt sleeves, he apologized for the overenthusiastic central heating system and made the brilliant observation that I would be much cooler without my winter coat. Foolishly, I concealed my predicament and insisted that I was perfectly comfortable. Besides, I believed that I could discreetly disengage the hook by wriggling my shoulders at an appropriate moment.

Every time he looked down at his papers, I wriggled. Unfortunately, he saw me. I could tell this by the increasingly uneasy expression in his eyes, the way he gradually shuffled his chair over to the far wall, and the relief in his voice when he said goodbye. I often wonder what he thought.

Anyway, those past memories, plus a dash of imagination, produced this picture. It demonstrates the body language of a selection of applicants, including myself. Twiggy's position illustrates my own feelings under such conditions. She's the one with the blue handbag. Poor cat, will she ever recover?

The confident character swaggering out of the office is Sam, the beautiful blue-pointed Siamese from up the lane. Sleek and refined, he doesn't approve of me and tosses his head when we meet.

Platform Four

I like the atmosphere of main line stations, where all kinds of people from different countries and walks of life rub shoulders. Some stride ahead of porters who push trolleys of monogrammed leather cases to first-class reserved seats. Others with bent knees and inflamed eyes shuffle their way to a plastic cup filled with tea, muttering as they drag their whole world behind them in a brown paper bag.

Most hurry with ant-like activity to individual platforms, often demonstratively laden by luggage, but rarely revealing the private, sometimes heavier, load inside their minds. The mixture of good and bad memories, mental images of well-known faces and places, the many personal hopes and apprehensions that nibble away inside all of us.

Bored children pull faces and giggle at exhausted bodies stretched on graffiti-covered wooden seats. People choose magazines and newspapers from the bright, busy bookstall, or read snippets over someone else's shoulder.

Doors swing open and bang closed. Time for greetings and goodbyes said with different tones in various tongues.

Whistles blow. The train lurches forward suddenly, and departs to a flourish of hands, handkerchiefs and blown kisses, rhythmically clicking its way into the distance.

I imagine the passengers in this painting are waiting for the Cornish Express because Mungo is there, complete with haversack and stowaway mice, returning home after that memorable month's absence.

Twiggy's there too, looking rather guiltily at that porter with the trolley. Oh Twiggy, what have you done!

❧ Swoop for a Scoop ❧

Here I was attempting to imagine what it might feel like to be a newly initiated VIP, constantly surrounded by a swooping flock of reporters and television cameras; as exposed as a scattering of corn in Trafalgar Square and sometimes as equally ill-fated. First scrutinized by a million hungry eyes, then pecked, devoured and enjoyed until eventually discarded like an empty husk while bored palates search for another flavour – a new and tastier morsel.

What do these exalted people think as they look down upon the army of poised pencils, the waving microphones and the myriad of clicking camera lenses?

One Too Many

I have mixed feelings about pet shops that display birds and animals alongside the accessories. My curiosity compels me to go inside even though I know I will only be upset by the appealing expression of the tiny creatures behind the bars.

It would help if the podgy mongrel puppies didn't wobble forward to fight for my attention and drum an enthusiastic message of welcome on the sides of the cage with their fat little tails.

I wish the kittens wouldn't accuse me of a callous nature with their sad eyes while they huddle together in a corner desperately trying to replace the warmth and security their mother once gave them.

The heart-rending memory of the latter on my last visit produced this picture. The kittens weren't really this colour; it was their expressions I wanted to paint, especially the one at the bottom of the pile who was nearly stifled by the weight of all the others.

🦋 Disco Madness 🦋

Here's my contribution to the current epidemic of disco fever. I thought I'd paint one of those dazzling discotheques where highly talented and energetic dancers in colourful costumes surrender their supple bodies to the music on brightly chequered floors.

Having said that, I'd better admit I've never been anywhere like this, certainly can't imagine myself in the gear and would like to ask some questions first. Does the admission ticket cover personal liability? Does the disc jockey really listen to the same loud music on his headphones or are they cleverly concealed ear muffs? Do the girls with long beaded hair lacerate their partner's body like a human rotary mower when they launch into a spontaneous treble pirouette? Or is that the reason why some of the men protect their jugular vein with a handkerchief?

In this imaginary disco, the character leaping over the exhausted body in the foreground is my memory of the pretty way Bobo used to skip across the grass with her tail shaped like a cup handle. This movement usually meant she had dug up the plants and was trying to run from the scene of the crime as nonchalantly as possible.

The spectators include a few feline acquaintances from my purely portrait-painting days – such as Rudolph, whose balletic movements earned him his name. (He's the one to the right of the front row, both paws up.) Then Suki, an old lady, young at heart. (She's front row again, watching the character with the handkerchief.) And Monty (front row, far left), a shy character whose big beautiful eyes regarded me suspiciously.

Remembering the Rush Hour

Between the age of eleven and thirteen I travelled on weekdays from my home in Hertfordshire to go to school in Chiswick. This picture stemmed from my memories of the claustrophobic crush that took place during the rush hour, but I also included some local characters on a day trip.

In the foreground is Sam – yes, another Sam – only this time a short-coated ginger-and-white that I will always remember with this dazed expression that resulted from overeating.

The fluffy ginger-and-white kittens looking through the window are Tigger and Marmalade; at one time abandoned, they were later adopted and thoroughly spoilt. I gave these two little imps an escort to keep them in order.

I see Twiggy has been on a shopping spree. There she is, straphanging while she daydreams.

The May Queen

I find that during different months the changing weather seems to complement different portions of Cornwall.

To me, the rugged north coastline looks best in the winter, when the sea crashes over the rocks at high tide with a thunderous warning to disrespectful onlookers, and at low tide the winds slice the dunes into curling yellow blankets that pursue each other in frenzied dance along the beach.

In contrast, the gently winding tree-lined creeks of the south coast respond to kind summer sunshine, and so does the colourful patchwork of fields in late August – especially the crackling corn, just before harvest.

My favourite month of all is May; when light showers followed by warm sun create a hazy curtain of steam in the narrow lanes, eventually clearing to reveal the true glory of moistened hedgerows filled with abundant wild flowers. Then I like to stroll through leafy valleys smelling the wood of the trees and the sweetly perfumèd bluebells, discovering the elaborate construction of a wild flower that at first glance looked so modest, or simply listening to the natural orchestra that assembles in unspoilt countryside.

This painting is based on such a valley – between Kehelland and the north coast. While I sketched a young cat played, seemingly oblivious of both time and my presence, its fur covered with sticky balls of goose-grass when it finally trotted off over the bridge, presumably homeward-bound.

The notice on the telegraph pole referred to a proposed site for a nuclear power station in St Ives Bay; pinned there as if to shake me from my peaceful contentment and remind me of the fears I share with many others in this complicated and nuclear-indulgent world.